Samuel Ferguson

Father Tom and the Pope

A night in the Vatican

Samuel Ferguson

Father Tom and the Pope
A night in the Vatican

ISBN/EAN: 9783744723565

Printed in Europe, USA, Canada, Australia, Japan

Cover: Foto ©Lupo / pixelio.de

More available books at **www.hansebooks.com**

Father Tom and the Pope,

OR

A Night in the Vatican.

NEW YORK:

A. SIMPSON & CO.,

1867.

PREFACE.

THERE are several questions which at this present time remain unsettled. One of them is, "*who invented gunpowder?*" Another is, which of them was it, Faust or Guttemberg, "*that invented printing?*" Another is, "*whether the Deity created nature, or nature created itself?*" That is a poser. Another is "*whether the original egg was the parent of the chicken, or the egg was the*

original ancestor of that celebrated feathered fowl?"
" *De novum ovum,*" says Xinctillios, " *inseperatum*
primero, cum possibilitas, et credentia, in meo judicio,
quam supra calcis phospas, qui est, in the bones of the
chicken." In other words, and to make it plain
to the reader, he, Xinctillios, cannot understand
how it is possible for human comprehension to
see a new laid egg, without permitting in his judgment the idea of phosphate of lime existing in the
osseous structure of the bones of the original
hen. St. Bardolphus entertains a contrary opinion,
"*Anam, aname, mona mike,*" says he, " *Barcelona bona*
strike," says he, " *harum scarum, wy frone whack !*"
(I give you the original Coptic) "*Harrico barrico,*
we won frac !"

Between these two contending opinions I have
nothing to say. The dogmas of the Roman Catho-

lic Church, and the *folatreries* of the philosophers of the high school of nature, differ so widely, that it is impossible for common sense to adopt either the one or the other—and the Greek Church on these points has given no decided opinion!

Such a dilemma presents itself when we come to consider the contents of this volume. Who wrote it? Some say, Lord Brougham; and some attribute it to the Duke of Wellington, who understood the Irish vernacular to a dot. I have a shrewd suspicion that Maginn, a high tory, although a good Roman Catholic, and one of the prominent contributors to *Blackwood*, lent his helping hand to it, if he were not the *real* author of it all? "Howandiver," to use a phrase of the author, let us look into the history of it.

Father Tom Maguire, a prominent Roman

Catholic priest in Killeshandra, Ireland, of the parish of Innismagrath, was one of the most celebrated men of his time. He was a splendid orator, trained at Maynooth; he was a high liver—everything consisting of meat and drink on his table was of the best; his wines were excellent, and he kept the best stable and the finest greyhounds in Ireland. He was a bold fox-hunter; rode over ditch, hedge and five-barred gate, and when his good Bishop interdicted these sports of the Irish clergy, says he, " I will give up my hunting," says he; " but if I must give up my greyhounds, there is a little Protestant parish church hard by waiting for me." Whether this threat had the desired effect is not known. It is said that he abjured his church and died a heretic. How much of this we can believe depends altogether upon the amount of our credulity.   It may be true, and, alas! it may

not!   Father Tom, as the great Roman Catho-

lic controversialist, was challenged to decide by

argument, the superiority of the Romish Church

over that of the Established Church of England,

by the Rev. Richard T. P. Pope, a clergyman of

the latter persuasion.   The controversy took place

in the Rotunda, at Dublin, about forty years ago.*

Crowds of spectators assembled to witness the

religious contest.   Of course the ladies, who always

take a great interest in religious disputations, were

present in great numbers.   The beauty and the

fashion, the graceful, the wise and the witty of

Dublin assembled to hear these knotty points dis-

cussed.   The Rev. Mr. Pope, who was a very

---

* In 1827.

learned scholar, but unfortunately a timid man, based his great argument upon the Bible itself. So long as he stood upon this ground his arguments were unassailable. But Father Tom, by one of those dexterous twists so well known in polemics, managed to get Pope to shift his ground from the Bible to the Fathers. The dispute, which had occupied several days, up to this time had been in favor of Pope, but when Father Maguire got him entangled in the Fathers, and hurled at him quotation after quotation from St. Austin, St. Chrysostom, and others—poor Pope, who knew very little of the Fathers, became so dumb-founderd that he was incapable of making a reply, and the victory rested with Father Tom. But after the controversy was over the Rev. Mr. Pope took up the Fathers, and to his surprise *could not find any*

of the quotations that Father Tom had cited !   Like a
true scholar, he published a book, exposing the falla-
cies of his antagonist.   But the time had gone by.
Few people cared to read it, fewer still had patience
to wade through laborious denials of the smart
sayings of Father Tom in the Rotunda ; the
sparkle was off—the champagne had ceased to
effervesce—and Mr. Pope never recovered the
ground he had lost.

Some years elapsed, and the Rev. Tresham D.
Gregg, of the Established Church, took up the
polemical cudgels to demolish the redoubtable
champion of the Romish Church. · He was just
such a man as his antagonist, vehement, loud
voiced—of the *ad captandum*, knock-down-and-
drag-out school.   Although not acknowledged by
the Church of England as the Goliath of its faith,

yet there is no doubt of the secret exultation of its clergy at his success. The challenge was accepted, and for a fortnight the Rotunda of Dublin rang with the verbal blows of these doughty combatants. Victory poised her scales, the contest hung in the balance. At last, one afternoon, after the battle of the day was over, Gregg raised his mighty arm high in the air, and said " that on the next day, the secrets of the confessional would be the subject of the discourse, and warned the ladies, "that no modest woman would appear, or could appear, while he revealed the secrets of that power-ful instrument of the Romish Church."

The consequences may be imagined. The hall was packed to overflowing by the gentler sex. Ladies of the Catholic persuasion, conscious of the inability of the orator to make his words good,

flocked to hear his discomfiture. Those of the
other persuasion were induced to come from a
laudable curiosity. The argument, if argument it
might be called, consisted on Gregg's part of that
style which Poe has properly denominated "the
awkward left arm of satire—*invective*." He had
caught Father Tom at single stick and paid him
off in his own way. There was of course no little
allusion to indelicate matters. After the argument
the Rev. Mr. Gregg had to be escorted to his
lodgings by a troop of dragoons. But at the close
of the debate he announced, that on the morrow
the subject would be *continued*. But on the fol-
lowing day Father Tom did not appear. The
victorious Gregg was cock of the walk ; the judgment went by default.

Whether any one among the speakers or listen-

ers became better Christians after the controversy,
is a question. It is doubtful whether Gregg or
Father Tom made or lost a single convert to
either faith.

"FATHER TOM AND THE POPE" first saw the
light in *Blackwood*, ten years after these controversies. It may have been written by Maginn,
who was a good Catholic, but it may truly be
said of him, that although he "loved the Church
much, he loved fun more." As a work of mere
wit it must take its place with some of the
brightest efforts of Rabelais, of Montaigne, or of
Pascal.

The ingenuity with which the conversation between the Pope and Father Tom is developed to
the reader, forms no little part of its felicitousness.
A hedge priest, one Michael Heffernan, of the

National School of Ballymacktaggart, is the inter-
locutor. This keeper of a ragged school, under
the shadow of an Irish hedge, is the exponent
of theological controversies that have shaken the
world! Happy satire! which like summer lightning, clears up the atmosphere, and makes even
the skies bright, blue, beautiful and buoyant. To
us! poor mortals! to whom a touch of nature
shakes the laughter out of us, or brings the
tears into our eyes, such books are the treasures
of our language.

If out of the sorrow and misery of this world,
wit has managed to alleviate one shade of
human suffering; if it has lifted up its hand
against tyranny; if it has sometimes by the pen
of Cervantes lessened the ridiculous power of a
so-called chivalry; or in the satires of Swift,

destroyed the prestige of hereditary birth; if it has done any good in this world, let so much good be accounted to it.

CHAPTER I.

HOW FATHER TOM WENT TO TAKE POT-LUCK AT THE VATICAN.

WHEN his Riv'rence was in Room, ov coorse the Pope axed him to take pot look wid him. More be token, it was on a Friday; but, for all that, there was plenty of mate; for the Pope gev himself an absolution from the fast on account ov the great company that was in it—at laste so I'm tould. Howandiver, there's no fast on the dhrink, anyhow—glory be to God!—and so, as they wor sitting, afther dinner, taking their sup together, says the Pope, says he, "Thomaus"—for the Pope, you know, spakes that away, all as one as one ov uz—"Thomaus *a lanna*," says he, "I'm tould you welt them English heretics out ov the face."

"You may say that," says his Riv'rence to him

2

again. "Be my sowl," says he, "if I put your
Holiness undher the table, you won't be the first
Pope I floored."

Well, his Holiness laughed like to split; for,
you know, Pope was the great Prodesan that
Father Tom put down upon Purgathory; and
ov coorse they knew all the ins and outs ov the
conthravarsy at Room. "Faix, Thomaus," says
he, smiling across the table at him mighty agreeable—"it's no lie what they tell me, that yourself
is the pleasant man over the dhrop ov good
liquor."

"Would you like to thry?" says his Riv'rence.

"Sure, and amn't I thrying all I can?" says
the Pope. "Sorra betther bottle ov wine's betuxt this and Salamancha, nor's there fornenst
you on the table; its raal Lachrymalchrystal,
every spudh ov it."

"It's mortial could," says Father Tom.

"Well, man alive," says the Pope, "sure and
here's the best ov good claret in the cut de-
canther."

"Not maning to make little ov the claret, your
Holiness," says his Riv'rence, "I would prefir

some hot wather and sugar, wid a glass of spirits through it, if convanient."

"Hand me over the bottle ov brandy," says the Pope to his head butler, "and fetch up the materi'ls," says he.

"Ah, then, your Holiness," says his Riv'rence, mighty eager, "maybe you'd have a dhrop ov the native in your cellar? Sure it's all one throuble," says he, "and, troth, I dunna how it is, but brandy always plays the puck wid my inthrails."

"'Pon my conscience, then," says the Pope, "it's very sorry I am, Misther Maguire," says he, "that it isn't in my power to plase you; for I'm sure and certaint that there's not as much whisky in Room this blessed minit as 'ud blind the eye ov a midge."

"Well, in troth, your Holiness," says Father Tom, "I knewn there was no use in axing; only," says he, "I didn't know how else to ex- queeze the liberty I tuck," says he, "ov bringing a small taste," says he, "ov the raal stuff," says he, hauling out an imperi'l quart bottle out ov his coat-pocket; "that never seen the face ov a gauger," says he, setting it down on the table

fornenst the Pope: "and if you'll jist thry the
full ov a thimble ov it, and if it doesn't rise the
cockles ov your Hóliness's heart, why, then, my
name," says he, "isn't Tom Maguire!" and wid
that he outs wid the cork.

Well, the Pope at first was going to get vexed
at Father Tom for fetching dhrink thataway in
his pocket, as if there wasn't lashins in the house:
so says he, "Misther Maguire," says he, "I'd
have you to comprehind the differ betuxt an
invitation to dinner from the successor ov Saint
Pether, and from a common mayur or a Prodesan
squireen that maybe hasn't liquor enough in his
cupboard to wet more nor his own heretical
whistle.   That may be the way wid them that
you visit in Leithrim," says he, "and in Ros-
common ; and I'd let you know the differ in the
prisint case," says he, "only that you're a champion of the Church and entitled to laniency.   So,"
says he, "as the liquor's come, let it stay.   And
in troth I'm curis myself," says he, getting mighty
soft when he found the delightful smell ov the
putteen, "in invistigating the composition ov dis-
tilled liquors; it's a branch of natural philos-

ophy," says he, taking up the bottle and putting it to his blessed nose. Ah! my dear, the very first snuff he got ov it, he cried out, the dear man: "Blessed Vargin, but it has the divine smell!" and crossed himself and the bottle half-a-dozen times running.

"Well, sure enough, it's the blessed liquor now," says his Riv'rence, "and so there can be no harm any way in mixing a dandy ov punch; and," says he, stirring up the materi'ls with his goolden muddler—for everything at the Pope's table, to the very schrew for drawing the corks, was ov vergin goold—"if I might make bould," says he, "to spake on so deep a subjic afore your Holiness, I think it 'ud considherably facilitate the invistigation ov its chemisthry and phwarmaceutics, if you'd jist thry the laste sup in life ov it inwardly."

"Well, then, suppose I do make the same expiriment," says the Pope, in a much more condiscinding way nor you'd have expected—and wid that he mixes himself a real stiff facer.

"Now, your Holiness," says Father Tom, "this bein' the first time you ever dispinsed them

chymicals," says he, " I'll just make bould to lay
down one rule of orthography," says he, "for
conwhounding them, *secundem mortem*."

" What's that ?" says the Pope.

" Put in the sperits first," says his Riv'rence ;
"and then put in the sugar ; and remember,
every dhrop ov wather you put in after that
spoils the punch."

"Glory be to God !" says the Pope, not mind-
ing a word Father Tom was saying. " Glory be
to God !" says he, smacking his lips. " I never
knewn what dhrink was afore," says he. "It
bates the Lachrymalchrystal out of the face !"
says he—" it's Necthar itself, it is, so it is !" says
he, wiping his epistolical mouth wid the cuff ov
his coat.

" 'Pon my secret honor," says his Riv'rence,
" I'm raally glad to see your Holiness set so
much to your satisfaction ; especially," says he,
" as, for fear ov accidents, I tuck the liberty ov
fetching the fellow ov that small vesshel," says
he, " in my other coat pocket. So divil a fear
ov our running dhry till the but-end ov the evening, anyhow," says he.

"Dhraw your stool in to the fire, Misther Maguire," says the Pope, "for faix," says he, "I'm bent on analysing the metaphwysics ov this phinomenon. Come, man alive, clear off," says he, "you're not dhrinking at all."

"Is it dhrink?" says his Riv'rence; "by Gorra, your Holiness," says he, "I'd dhrink wid you till the cows'ud be coming home in the morning."

So wid that they tackled to, to the second fugee a piece, and fell into larned discourse. But it's time for me now to be off to the lecthir at the Boord. Oh my sorra light upon ye, Docther Whately, wid your pilitical econimy and your hydherastatics! What the *dioul* use has a poor hedge-master like me wid such deep larning as is only fit for the likes of them two that I left over their second tumbler? Howandiver, wishing I was like them, in regard ov the sup of dhrink, anyhow, I must break off my norration for the prisint; but when I see you again, I'll tell you how Father Tom made a hare ov the Pope that evening, both in theology and the cube root.

CHAPTER II.

HOW FATHER TOM SACKED HIS HOLINESS IN THEOLOGY AND LOGIC.

WELL, the lecthir's over, and I'm kilt out and out. My bitther curse upon the man that invinted the same Boord! I thought ons't I'd fadomed the say ov throuble; and that was when I got through fractions at Ould Mat Kavanagh's school, in Firdramore—God be good to poor Mat's sowl, though he did deny the cause the day he suffered! but it's fluxions itself we're set to bottom now, sink or shwim! May I never die if my head isn't as throughother as anything wid their ordinals and cardinals—and, begob, its all nothing to the econimy lecthir that I have got to go to at two o'clock. Howandiver, I mustn't forget that we left his Riv'rence and his Holiness sitting fornenst one another in the parlor ov the Vatican, jist afther mixing their second tumbler.

When they had got well down into the same,
they fell, as I was telling you, into larned discourse.   For, you see, the Pope was curious to
find out whether Father Tom was the great theo-
loginall that people said ; and says he, " Misther
Maguire," says he, "what answer do you make to
the heretics when they quote them passidges agin
thransubstantiation out ov the Fathers ?" says he.

"Why," says his Riv'rence, "as there should
be no sich passidges I make myself mighty aisy
about them ; but if you want to know how I dis-
pose ov them," says he, "just repate one ov
them," says he, "and I'll show you how to
catapomphericate it in two shakes."

"Why, then," says the Pope, "myself disre-
mimbers the particlar passidges they alledge out
of them old felleys," says he, " though sure
enough they're more numerous nor edifying—so
we'll jist suppose that a heretic was to find sich a
saying as this in Austin, ' Every sinsible man
knows that thransubstantiation is a lie '—or this
out of Tertullian or Plutarch, ' the Bishop ov
Room is a common imposther,' now tell me,
could you answer him ?"

3

"As easy as kiss," says his Riv'rence. "In the first, we're to understand that the exprission, 'Every sinsible man,' signifies simply, 'Every man that judges by his nath'ral sinses;' and we all know that nobody folleying them seven deludhers could ever find out the mysthery that's in it, if somebody didn't come in to his assistance wid an eighth sinse, which is the only sinse to be depended on, being the sinse ov the Church. So that, regarding the first quotation which your Holiness has supposed, it makes clane for us, and tee-totally agin the heretics."

"That's the explanation sure enough," says his Holiness; "and now what div you say to my being a common imposther?"

"Faix, I think," says his Riv'rence, "wid all submission to the better judgment ov the learned father that your Holiness has quoted, he'd have been a thrifle nearer the truth, if he had said that the Bishop ov Room is the grand imposther and top-sawyer in that line over us all."

"What do you mane?" says the Pope, getting quite red in the face.

"What would I mane," says his Riv'rence, as

composed as a docther ov physic, "but that your
Holiness is at the head ov all them—troth I had
a'most forgot I wasn't a bishop myself," says he,
(the deludher was going to say, as the head ov all
us)—"that has the gift ov laying on hands. For
sure," says he, "imposther and *imposithir* is all
one, so you're only to undherstand *manuum*, and
the job is done. Awouich!" says he, "if any
heretic 'ud go for to cast up sich a passidge as that
agin me, I'd soon give him a lesson in the p'lite
art ov cutting a stick to welt his own back wid."

"'Pon my epostolical word," says the Pope,
"you've cleared up them two pints in a most
satisfactory manner."

"You. see," says his Riv'rence—by this time
they wor mixing their third tumbler--" the writ-
ings ov them Fathers is to be thrated wid great
veneration ; and it 'ud be the height of presump-
tion in any one to sit down to interpret them
widout providing himself wid a genteel assortment
ov the best figures ov rhetoric, sich as mettonymy,
hyperbol, cattychraysis, prolipsis, mettylipsis, superbaton, pollysyndreton, hustheronprotheron,
prosodypeia and the, like, in ordher that he may

never be at a loss for shuitable sintiments when
he comes to their high-flown passidges. For
unless we thrate them Fathers liberally to a handsome allowance ov thropes and figures, they'd set
up heresy at ons't, so they would."

"It's thrue for you," says the Pope; "the
figures ov spache is the pillars ov the Church."

"Bedad," says his Riv'rence, "I dunna what
we'd do widout them at all."

"Which one do you prefir?" says the Pope;
"that is," says he, "which figure ov spache do
you find most usefullest when you're hard set?"

"Metaphour's very good," says his Riv'rence,
"and so's mettonymy—and I've known prosodypeia
stand to me at a pinch mighty well—but for a con-
stancy, superbaton's the figure for my money.
Divil be in me," says he, "but I'd prove black
white as fast as a horse 'ud throt wid only a good
stock ov superbaton."

"Faix," says the Pope, wid a sly look, "you'd
need to have it backed, I judge, wid a small taste
ov assurance."

"Well now, jist for that word," says his Riv'-
rence, "I'll prove it widout aither one or other.

Black," says he, "is one thing and white is another thing. You don't conthravene ʼthat ? But
every thing is aither one thing or another thing;
I defy the apostle Paul to get over that dilemma.
Well ! If any thing be one thing, well and good;
but if it be another thing, then it's plain it isn't
both things, and so can't be two things—nobody
can deny that. But what can't be two things
must be one thing—*Ergo*, whether it's one thing
or another thing it's all one. But black is one
thing and white is another thing—*Ergo*, black
and white is all one. *Quod erat demonsthrandum.*"

"Stop a bit," says the Pope, "I can't althe-
gither give in to your second minor—no—your
second major," says he, and he stopped. "Faix,
then," says he, getting confused, "I don't rightly
remimber where it was exactly that I thought I
seen the flaw in your premises. Howsomdiver,"
says he, "I don't deny that it's a good conclusion,
and one that 'ud be ov materi'l service to the
Church if it was dhrawn wid a little more distinct-
iveness."

"I'll make it as plain as the nose on your
Holiness's face, by superbaton," says his Riv'-

rence. "My adversary says black is not another
color, that is, white! Now, that's jist a parallel
passidge wid the one out ov Tartullian that me
and Hayes smashed the heretics on in Clarendon
sthreet, 'This is my body—that is, the figure ov
my body.' That's a superbaton, and we showed
that it oughtn't to be read that way at all, but
this way, 'This figure ov my body *is* my body.'
Jist so wid my adversary's proposition, it mustn't
be undherstood the way it reads, by no manner ov
manes; but it's to be taken this way—' Black—
that is, white, is not another color '—green, if you
like, or orange, by dad, for anything I care, for
my case is proved. 'Black,' that is, 'white,' lave
out the ' that,' by sinnalayphy, and you have the
orthodox conclusion, ' Black is white,' or by con-
varsion, 'White is black.'"

"It's as clear as mud," says the Pope.

"Begad," says his Riv'rence, "I'm in great
humor for disputin' to-night. I wisht your Holiness was a heretic jist for two minutes," says he,
"till you'd see the flaking I'd give you !"

"Well, then, for the fun o' the thing, suppose
me my namesake, if you like," says the Pope,

laughing, "though, by Jayminy," says he, "he's not one that I take much pride out ov."

"Very good—divil a betther joke ever I had," says his Riv'rence. "Come, then, Misther Pope," says he, "hould up that purty face ov yours, and answer me this question. Which 'ud be the biggest lie, if I said I seen a turkey-cock lying on the broad ov his back, and picking the stars out ov the sky, or if I was to say that I seen a gandher in the same interestin' posture, raycreating himself wid similar asthronomical expiriments? Answer me that, you ould swaddler?" says he.

"How durst you call me a swaddler, sir," says the Pope, forgetting, the dear man, the part that he was acting.

"Don't think for to bully me!" says his Riv'rence, "I always daar to spake the truth, and it's well known that you're nothing but a swaddling ould sinner of a saint," says he, never letting on to persave that his Holiness had forgot what they were agreed on.

"By all that's good," says the Pope, "I often hard ov the imperance ov you Irish afore," says he, "but I never expected to be called a saint in

my own house either by Irishman or Hottentot.
I'll till you what, Misther Maguire," says he, " if
you can't keep a civil tongue in your head, you
had betther be walking off wid yourself; for I beg
lave to give you to undherstand, that it won't be
for the good ov your health if you call me by sich
an outprobrious epithet again," says he.

   " Oh, indeed ! then things is come to a purty
pass," says his Riv'rence (the dear funny soul
that he ever was !) "when the likes of you com-
pares one of the Maguires ov Tempo wid a wild
Ingine !   Why, man alive, the Maguires was
kings ov Fermanagh three thousand years afore
your grandfather, that was the first of your breed
that ever wore shoes and stockings" (I'm bound to
say, in justice to the poor Prodesan, that this was
all spoken by his Riv'rence by way ov a figure ov
spache), " was sint his Majesty's arrand to culti-
vate the friendship of Prince Lee Boo in Botteney
Bay !   Oh Bryan, dear," says he, letting on to
cry, "if you were alive to hear a *boddagh Sassenagh*
like this casting up his counthry to one ov the
name ov Maguire !"

   " In the name ov God," says the Pope, very

solemniously, "what *is* the meaning ov all this at all at all?" says he.

"Sure," says his Riv'rence, whispering to him across the table, "sure you know we're acting a conthravarsy, and you tuck the part of the Prodesan champion. You wouldn't be angry wid me, I'm sure, for sarving out the heretic to the best ov my ability."

"Oh begad, I had forgot," says the Pope, the good-natured ould crethur; "sure enough you were only taking your part, as a good Milesian Catholic ought, agin the heretic Sassenagh. Well," says he, "fire away now, and I'll put up wid as many conthrovarsial compliments as you plase to pay me."

"Well, then, answer me my question, you sanctimonious ould dandy," says his Riv'rence.

"In troth, then," says the Pope, "I dunna which 'ud be the biggest lie: to my mind," says he, "the one appears to be about as big a bounce as the other."

"Why, then, you poor simpleton," says his Riv'rence, "don't you persave that, forbye the advantage the gandher 'ud have in the length ov

4

his neck, it 'ud be next to onpossible for the
turkey-cock lying thataway to see what he was
about, by rason ov his djollars and other accouth-
rements hanging back over his eyes? The one
about as big a bounce as the other! Oh, you
misforthunate crethur! if you had ever larned
your A B C in theology, you'd have known that
there's a differ betuxt them two lies so great, that,
begad, I wouldn't wondher if it 'ud make a balance ov five years in purgathory to the sowl that
ud be in it. Ay, and if it wasn't that the Church
is too liberal entirely, so she is, it 'ud cost his
heirs and succissors betther nor ten pounds to
have him out as soon as the other. Get along,
man, and take half-a-year at dogmatical theology:
go and read your Dens, you poor dunce, you!"

"Raaly," says the Pope, "you're making the
heretic's shoes too hot to hould me. I wondher
how the Prodesans can stand afore you at all."

"Don't think to delude me," says his Riv'rence,
"don't think to back out ov your challenge now,"
says he, "but come to the scratch like a man, if
you are a man, and answer me my question.
What's the rason, now, that Julius Cæsar and the

Vargin Mary was born upon the one day?—
answer me that, if you wouldn't be hissed off the
platform!"

Well, my dear, the Pope couldn't answer it,
and he had to acknowledge himself sacked. Then
he axed his Riv'rence to tell him the rason himself; and Father Tom communicated it to him in
Latin. But as that is a very deep question, I
never hard what the answer was, except that I'm
tould it was so mysterious, it made the Pope's
hair stand on end.

But there's two o'clock, and I'll be late for the
lecthir.

CHAPTER III.

HOW FATHER TOM MADE A HARE OF HIS HOLINESS IN LATIN.

OH, Dochter Whately, Docther Whately, I'm sure I'll never die another death if I don't die aither of consumption or production! I ever and always thought that asthronomy was the hardest science that was till now—and it's no lie I'm telling you, the same asthronomy is a tough enough morsel to break a man's fast upon—and geolidgy is middling and hard too—and hydherastatics is no joke; but ov all the books ov science that ever was opened and shut, that book upon Pilitical Econimy lifts the pins! Well, well, if they wait till they persuade me that taking a man's rints out ov the counthry, and spinding them in forrain parts isn't doing us out ov the same, they'll wait a long time in troth. But you're waiting, I see, to hear how his Riv'rence and his Holiness got on after finishing the disputation I was telling you ov. Well, you see, my dear, when the Pope found he couldn't hould a candle to Father Tom in theology and logic, he thought he'd take the shine out ov him in Latin anyhow; so says he, "Misther Maguire," says he, "I quite agree wid you that it's not lucky for us to be spaking on them deep subjects in sich langidges as the evil spirits is acquainted wid; and," says he, "I think it 'ud be no harm for us to spake from this out in Latin," says he, "for fraid the devil 'ud undherstand what we are saying."

"Not a hair I care," says Father Tom, "whether he undherstands what we're saying or not, so long as we keep off that last pint we wor discussing, and one or two others. List'ners never heard good ov themselves," says he; "and if Belzhebub takes anything amiss that aither you or me says in regard ov himself or his faction, let him stand forrid like a man, and, never fear, I'll give him his answer. Howandiver, if it's for a taste ov classic conversation you are, just to put

us in mind ov ould Cordarius," says he, "here's
at you ;" and wid that he lets fly at his Holiness
wid his health in Latin.

"Vesthræ Sanctitatis salutem volo !" says he.

"Vesthræ Revirintiæ salubritati bibo !" says
the Pope to him again (faith, it's no joke, I
tell you, to remimber sich a power ov larning).
"Here's to you wid the same," says the Pope, in
the raal Ciceronian.   "Nunc poculum alterhum
imple," says he.

"Cum omni jucunditate in vita," says his Riv'-
rence.   "Cum summâ concupiscintiâ et animosi-
tate," says he ; as much as to say : "Wid all the
veins ov my heart, I'll do that same ;" and so, wid
that, they mixed their fourth gun a piece.

"Aqua vitæ vesthra sane est liquor admirabilis,"
says the Pope.

"Verum est pro te—it's thrue for you," says his
Riv'rence, forgetting the idyim ov the Latin phraw-
seology, in a manner.

"Prava est tua Latinitas, domine," says the
Pope, finding fault like wid his etymology.

"Parva culpa mihi," "small blame to me, that
is," says his Riv'rence ; "nam multum laboro in

partibus interioribus," says he—the dear man!
that never was at a loss for an excuse!

"Quid tibi incommodi?" says the Pope, axing
him what ailed him.

"Habesne id quod Anglice vocamus, a looking-
glass," says his Riv'rence.

"Immo, habeo speculum splendidissimum subther operculum pyxidis hujus starnutatoriæ," says
the Pope, pulling out a beautiful goold snuff-box,
wid a looking-glass in under the lid; "Subther
operculum pyxidis hujus starnutatorii—no—starnutatoriæ—quam dono accepi ab Archi-duce Aus-
thriaco siptuagisima prætheritâ," says he; as much
as to say that he got the box in a prisint from the
Queen of Spain last Lint, if I rightly remimber.

Well, Father Tom laughed like to burst. At
last says he, "Pather Sancte," says he, "sub
errore jaces. 'Looking-glass' apud nos habet sig-
nificationem quamdam peculiarem ex tempore diei
dependentem"—there was a sthring ov accusatives
for yez!—"nam mane speculum sonat," says he,
"post prandium vero mat—mat—mat"—sorra be
in me but I disremimber the classic appellivation
ov the same article. Howandiver, his Riv'rence

went on explaining himself in such a way as no
scholar could mistake. " Vesica mea," says he,
"ab illo ultimo eversore distenditur, donec similis
est rumpere. Verbis apertis," says he, " Vesthræ
Sanctitatis præsentia salvata, aquam facere valde
desidhero."

" Ho, ho, ho !" says the Pope, grabbing up his
box ; " si inquinavisses meam pyxidem, excimni-
cari debuisses. Hillo, Anthony," says he to his
head butler, " fetch Misther Maguire a——"

" You spoke first !" says his Riv'rence, jumping
off his sate : " You spoke first in the vernacular.
I take Misther Anthony to witness," says he.

" What else would you have me to do ?" says
the Pope, quite dogged like to see himself bate
thataway at his own waypons. " Sure," says he,
" Anthony wouldn't undherstand a B from a bull's
foot, if I spoke to him any other way."

" Well, then," says his Riv'rence, in considher-
ation ov the needcessity," says he, " I'll let you
off for this time ; but mind, now, afther I say
præstho, the first of us that spakes a word of English is the hare—*præstho!*"

Neither ov them spoke for near a minit, con-

sidhering wid themselves how they wor to begin
sich a great thrial ov shkill.   At last says the
Pope—the blessed man ! only think how 'cute it
was ov him !—" Domine Maguire," says he,
" valde desidhero, certiorem fieri de significatione
istius verbi *eversor* quo jam jam usus es"—(well,
surely I *am* the boy for the Latin !)

" *Eversor*, id est cyathus," says his Riv'rence,
" nam apud nos *tumbleri*, seu eversores, dicti sunt
ab evertendo ceremonian inter amicos; non, ut
Temperantiæ Societatis frigidis fautoribus placet,
ab evertendis ipsis potatoribus."   (It's not every
masther unher the Boord, I tell you, could carry
such a car-load ov the dead langidges.)   "In agro
vero Louthiano et Midensi," says he, " nomine
gaudent quodam secundum linguam Anglicanam
significante bombardam seu tormentum ; quia ex
eis tanquam ex telis jaculatoriis liquorem faucibus
immitere solent.   Etiam inter hæreticos illos
melanostomos " (that was a touch of Greek),
" Presbyterianos Septentrionales, qui sunt terri-
biles potatores, Cyathi dicti sunt *faceres*, et dimidium Cyathi *hæf-a-glessus*.   Dimidium Cyathi vero
apud Metropolitanos Hibernicos dicitur *dandy*."—
5

"En verbum Anglicanum!" says the Pope,
clapping his hands—"leporem te fecisti;" as
much as to say that he had made a hare ov himself.

"*Dandæus, dandæus*, verbum erat," says his
Riv'rence—oh, the dear man, but it's himself that
was handy ever and always at getting out ov a
hobble—"*dandæus* verbum erat," says he, "quod
dicturus eram, cum me intherpillavisti."

"Ast ego dico," says the Pope, very sharp,
"quod verbum erat *dandy*."

"Per tibicinem qui coram Mose modulatus
est," says his Riv'rence, "id flagellat mundum!
Dandæus dixi, et tu dicis *dandy;* ergo tu es lepus,
non ego—Ah, ha!   Saccavi vesthram Sanctita-
tem!"

"Mendacium est!" says the Pope, quite forgetting himself, he was so mad at being sacked
before the sarvints.

Well, if it hadn't been that his Holiness was in
it, Father Tom 'ud have given him the contints
of his tumbler betuxt the two eyes for calling him
a liar; and, in troth, it's very well it was in Latin
the offince was conveyed, for, if it had been in the

vernacular, there's no saying what 'ud ha' been the consequence. His Riv'rence was mighty angry anyhow.—" Tu senex lathro," says he, " quomodo audes me mendacem prædicare ?"

" Et tu, sacrilege nebulo," says the Pope, " quomodo audacitatem habeas, me Dei in terris vicarium, lathronem conviciari ?"

" Interroga circumcirca," says his Riv'rence.

" Abi ex ædibus meis," says the Pope.

" Abi tu in malem crucem," says his Riv'rence.

" Excomunicabo te," says the Pope.

" Diabolus curat," says his Riv'rence.

" Anathema sis," says the Pope.

" Oscula meum pod," says his Riv'rence—but, my dear, afore he could finish what he was going to say, the Pope broke out into the vernacular, " Get out o' my house, you reprobate !" says he, in sich a rage that he could contain himself widin the Latin no longer.

"Ha, ha, ha!—ho, ho, ho!" says his Riv'rence. " Who's the hare now, your Holiness ? Oh, by this and by that, I've sacked you clane ! Clane and clever I've done it, and no mistake ! You see what a bit ov desate will do wid the wisest,

your Holiness—sure it was joking I was, on purpose to aggravate you—all's fair, you know, in
love, law, and conthravarsy.   In troth if I'd
thought you'd have taken it so much to heart, I'd
have put my head into the fire afore I'd have said
a word to offind you," says he, for he seen that
the Pope was very vexed. . "Sure, God forbid ·
that I'd say anything agin your Holiness, barring
it was in fun : for arn't you the father ov the
faithful, and the thrue vicar ov God upon earth ?
And amn't I ready to go down on my two knees
this blessed minit and beg your epostolical pardon
for every word that I said to your displasement ?"

"Are you in arnest that it is in fun you wor ?"
says the Pope.

"May I never die if I amn't," says his Riv'-
rence.   "It was all to provoke your Holiness to
commit a brache ov the Latin that I tuck the
small liberties I did," says he.

"I'd have you to take care," says the Pope,
" how you take sich small liberties again, or maybe you'll provoke me to commit a brache ov the
pace."

"Well, and if I did," said his Riv'rence, "I

know a sartan preparation ov chymicals that's very
good for curing a brache either in Latinity or frind-
ship."

"What's that?" says the Pope, quite mollified,
and sitting down again at the table that he had ris
from in the first pluff ov his indignation. "What's
that?" says he, "for, 'pon my Epistolical 'davy,
I think it 'udn't be asy to bate this miraclous mixthir that we've been thrying to anilize this two
hours back," says he, taking a mighty scientifical
swig out ov the bottom ov his tumbler.

"It's good for a beginning," says his Riv'rence:
"it lays a very nate foundation for more sarious
operation: but we're now arrived at a pariod ov
the evening when its time to proceed wid our
shuperstructhure by compass and square, like free
and excipted masons as we both are."

My time's up for the present; but I'll tell you
the rest in the evening at home.

CHAPTER IV.

HOW FATHER TOM AND HIS HOLINESS DISPUTED
IN METAPHYSICS AND ALGEBRA.

GOD be wid the time when I went to the clas-
sical seminary ov Firdramore! when I'd bring my
sod o' turf undher my arm, and sit down on my
shnug boss o' straw, wid my back to the masther
and my shins to the fire, and score my sum in
Dives's denominations or the double rule o' three,
or play fox-and-geese wid purty Jane Cruise that
sat next me, as plisantly as the day was long, widout any one so much as saying, " Mikey Heffernan, what's that you're about?"—for ever since I
was in the one lodge wid poor ould Mat I had my
own way in his school as free as ever I had in my
mother's shebeen. God be wid them days, I say
again, for its althered times wid me, I judge, since
I got under Carlisle and Whately. Sich sthrict-
ness! sich ordher! sich dhrilling, and lecthiring,
and tuthoring as they do get on wid! I wisht to

gracious the one-half ov their rules and rigilations was sunk in the say. And they're getting so sthrict, too, about having fair play for the heretic childher! We've to have no more schools in the chapels, nor masses in the schools. Oh, by this and by that it'll never do at all! The ould plan was twenty times betther; and, for my own part, if it wasn't that the clargy supports them in a manner, and the grant's a thing not easily done widout these hard times, I'd see if I couldn't get a sheltered spot nigh-hand the chapel, and set up again on the good ould principle: and faix, I think our Metropolitan 'ud stand to me, for I know that his Grace's motto was ever and always, that " Ignorance is the thrue mother of piety."

But I'm running away from my norration entirely, so I am. " You'll plase to ordher up the housekeeper, then," says Father Tom to the Pope, " wid a pint ov sweet milk in a skillet, and the bulk ov her fist ov butther, along wid a dust ov soft sugar in a saucer, and I'll show you the way ov producing a decoction that, I'll be bound, will hunt the thirst out ov every nook and corner in your Holiness's blessed carcidge."

The Pope ordhered up the ingredients, and they were brought in by the head butler.

"That'll not do at all," says his Riv'rence, "the ingredients won't combine in due proportion unless ye do as I bid yez. Send up the house-keeper," says he, "for a faymale hand is ondis-pinsably necessary to produce the adaptation ov the particles and the concurrence ov the corpuscles, without which you might boil till morning, and never fetch the cruds off ov it."

Well, the Pope whispered to his head butler, and by-and-by up there comes an ould faggot ov a *Caillean*, that was enough to frighten a horse from his oats.

"Don't thry for to desave me," says his Riv'-rence, "for it's no use, I tell yez. Send up the housekeeper, I bid yez: I seen her presarving gooseberries in the panthry as I came up: she has eyes as black as a sloe," says he, "and cheeks like the rose in June; and sorra taste ov this celestial mixthir shall crass the lips ov man or mortial this blessed night till she stirs the same up wid her own delicate little finger."

"Misther Maguire," says the Pope, "it's very

unproper ov you to spake that way ov my housekeeper: I won't allow it, sir."

"Honor bright, your Holiness," says his Riv'-
rence, laying his hand on his heart.

"Oh, by this and by that, Misther Maguire,"
says the Pope, "I'll have none ov your insiniva-
tions: I don't care who sees my whole household,"
says he; "I don't care if all the faymales undher
my roof was paraded down the High Street ov
Room," says he.

"Oh, it's plain to be seen how little you care
who sees them," says his Riv'rence. "You're
afeared, now, if I was to see your housekeeper,
that I'd say she was too handsome."

"No, I'm not!" says the Pope; "I don't care
who sees her," says he. "Anthony," says he to
the head butler, "bid Eliza throw her apron over
her head, and come up here." Wasn't that stout
in the blessed man? Well, my dear, up she
came, stepping like a three-year-old, and blushing
like the break o' day: for though her apron
was thrown over her head as she came forrid,
till you could barely see the tip ov her chin—
more be token there was a lovely dimple in it,

6

as I've been tould—yet she let it shlip a bit
to one side, by chance like, jist as she got for-
ninst the fire, and if she wouldn't have given his
Riv'rence a shot if he hadn't been a priest, it's no
matther.

"Now, my dear," says he, "you must take that
skillet, and hould it over the fire till the milk
comes to a blood-hate; and the way you'll know
that will be by stirring it ons't or twice wid the
little finger ov your right hand, afore you put in
the butther: not that I misdoubt," says he, "but
that the same finger's fairer nor the whitest milk
that ever came from the tit."

"None ov your deludhering talk to the young
woman, sir," says the Pope, mighty stern. "Stir
the posset as he bids you, Eliza, and then be off
wid yourself," says he.

"I beg your Holiness's pardon ten thousand
times," says his Riv'rence; "I'm sure I meant
nothing onproper; I hope I'm uncapable ov any
sich dirilection ov my duty," says he. "But,
marciful Saver!" he cried out, jumping up on a
suddent, "look behind you, your Holiness—I'm
blest but the room's on fire!"

Sure enough the candle fell down that minit, and was near setting fire to the windy-curtains, and there was some bustle, as you may suppose, getting things put to rights. And now I have to tell you ov a raally onpleasant occurrence. If I was a Prodesan that was in it, I'd say that while the Pope's back was turned, Father Tom made free wid the two lips ov Miss Eliza; but, upon my conscience, I believe it was a mere mistake that his Holiness fell into on account of his being an ould man, and not having aither his eyesight or his hearing very parfect. At any rate it can't be denied but that he had a sthrong imprission that sich was the case; for he wheeled about as quick as thought, jist as his Riv'rence was sitting down, and charged him wid the offince plain and plump. "Is it kissing my housekeeper before my face you are, you villain?" says he. "Go down out o' this," says he to Miss Eliza; "and do you be packing off wid you," he says to Father Tom, "for it's not safe, so it isn't, to have the likes ov you in a house where there's temptation in your way."

"Is it me?" says his Riv'rence; "why, what

would your Holiness be at, at all? Sure I wasn't
doing no sich thing."

"Would you have me doubt the evidence ov
my sinses?" says the Pope; "would you have
me doubt the testimony ov my eyes and ears?"
says he.

"Indeed I would so," says his Riv'rence, "if
they pretind to have informed your Holiness of
any sich foolishness."

"Why," says the Pope, "I seen you afther
kissing Eliza as plain as I see the nose on your
face; I heard the smack you gave her as plain as
ever I heard thundher."

"And how do you know whether you see the
nose on my face or not?" says his Riv'rence;
"and how do you know whether what you thought
was thundher, was thundher at all? Them opera-
tions of the sinses," says he, "comprises only
particular corporayal emotions, connected wid
sartin confused perciptions called sinsations, and
isn't to be depended upon at all. If we were to
follow them blind guides, we might jist as well
turn heretics at ons't. 'Pon my secret word, your
Holiness, it's naither charitable nor orthodox ov

you to set up the testimony ov your eyes and
ears agin the character ov a clergyman. And
now, see how aisy it is to explain all them phwen-
omena that perplexed you. I ris and went over
beside the young woman because the skillet was
boiling over, to help her to save the dhrop ov
liquor that was in it; and as for the noise you
heard, my dear man, it was neither more nor less
nor myself dhrawing the cork out ov this blissid
bottle."

" Don't offer to thrape that upon me !" says
the Pope ; "here's the cork in the bottle still, as
tight as a wedge."

" I beg your pardon," says his Riv'rence,
"that's not the cork at all," says he ; " I dhrew
the cork a good two minits ago, and it's very
purtily spitted on the end ov this blessed cork-
shcrew at this prisint moment; howandiver you
can't see it, because it's only its raal prisence that's
in it. But that appearance that you call a cork,"
says he, " is nothing but the outward spacies and
external qualities ov the cortical nathur. Them's
nothing but the accidents ov the cork that you're
looking at and handling ; but, as I tould you

afore, the real cork's dhrew, and is here prisint on
the end ov this nate little insthrument, and it was
the noise I made in dhrawing it, and nothing else,
that you mistook for the sound ov the *pogue*."

You know there was no conthravening what he
said ; and the Pope couldn't openly deny it.
Howandiver he thried to pick a hole in it this
way.   " Granting," says he, " that there is the
differ you say betuxt the reality ov the cork and
them cortical accidents, and that it's quite possible,
as you allidge, that the thrue cork is really prisint
on the end ov the shcrew, while the accidents
keep the mouth ov the bottle stopped—still,"
says he, " I can't undherstand, though willing to
acquit you, how the dhrawing ov the real cork,
that's onpalpable and widout accidents, could produce the accident ov that sinsible explosion I
heard jist now."

" All I can say," says his Riv'rence, "is, that
I'm sinsible it was a raal accident, anyhow."

"Ay," says the Pope, "The kiss you gev Eliza,
you mane."

" No," says his Riv'rence, " but the report I
made."

"I don't doubt you," says the Pope.

"No cork could be dhrew with less noise," says his Riv'rence.

"It would be hard for anything to be less nor nothing, barring algebra," says the Pope.

"I can prove to the conthrary," says his Riv'rence. "This glass ov whisky is less nor that tumbler ov punch, and that tumbler ov punch is nothing to this jug of *scaltheen*."

"Do you judge by superficial misure or by the liquid contents?" says the Pope.

"Don't stop me betuxt my premisses and my conclusion," says his Riv'rence; "*Ergo*, this glass ov whisky is less nor nothing; and for that raison I see no harm in life in adding it to the contents ov the same jug, just by way ov a frost-nail."

"Adding what's less nor nothing," says the Pope, "is subthraction according to algebra; so here goes to make the rule good," says he, filling his tumbler wid the blessed stuff, and sitting down again at the table, for the anger didn't stay two minutes on him, the good-hearted ould sowl.

"Two minuses makes one plus," says his Riv'rence, as ready as you plase, "and that'll account for the increased daycrement I mane to take the liberty ov producing in the same mixed quantity," says he, follying his Holiness's epistolical example.

"By all that's good," says the Pope, "that's the best stuff I ever tasted; you call it a mixed quantity, but I say it's prime."

"Since it's ov the first ordher, then," says his Riv'rence, "we'll have the less deffeequilty in reducing it to a simple equation."

"You'll have no fractions at my side, anyhow," says the Pope. "Faix, I'm afeard," says he, "it's only too aisy ov solution our sum is like to be."

"Never fear for that," says his Riv'rence, "I've a good stock ov surds here in the bottle; for I tell you it will take us a long time to exthract the root ov it, at the rate we're going on."

"What makes you call the blessed quart an irrational quantity?" says the Pope.

"Becase it's too much for one, and too little for two," says his Riv'rence.

"Clear it ov its co-efficient, and we'll thry," says the Pope.

"Hand me over the exponent, then," says his Riv'rence.

"What's that?" says the Pope.

"The schrew, to be sure," says his Riv'rence.

"Sure the cork's dhrew," says the Pope.

"But the sperits can't get out on account of the accidents that's stuck in the neck ov the bottle," says his Riv'rence.

"Accident ought to be passable to sperit," says the Pope, "and that makes me suspect that the reality ov the cork's in it afther all."

"That's a barony-masia," says his Riv'rence, "and I'm not bound to answer it. But the fact is, that it's the accidents ov the sperits too that's in it, and the reality's passed out through the cortical spacies as you say; for, you may have observed, we've both been in raal good sperits ever since the cork was dhrawn, and where else would the raal sperits come from if they would't come out ov the bottle?"

"Well, then," says the Pope, "since we've got the reality, there's no use throubling ourselves wid the accidents."

"Oh, begad," says his Riv'rence, "the accidents is very essential too; for a man may be in the best of good sperits, as far as his immaterial

7   •

part goes, and yet need the accidental qualities ov
good liquor to hunt the sinsible thirst out ov him."
So he dhraws the cork in earnest, and sets about
brewing the other skillet ov *scaltheen;* but, faix,
he had to get up the ingredients this time by the
hands ov ould Molly; though devil a taste ov her
little finger he'd let widin a yard ov the same decoction.

But, my dear, here's the *Freeman's Journal,* and
we'll see what's the news afore we finish the resid-
uary proceedings ov their two Holinesses.

CHAPTER V.

THE REASON WHY FATHER TOM WAS NOT MADE A CARDINAL.

HURROO, my darlings!—didn't I tell you it 'ud never do? Success to bould John Tuam and the old siminary of Firdramore! Oh, more power to your Grace every day you rise, 'tis you that has broken their Boord into shivers undher your feet! Sure, and isn't it a proud day for Ireland, this blessed feast ov the chair ov Saint Pether? Isn't Carlisle and Whately smashed to pieces, and their whole college ov swaddling teachers knocked into smidhereens. John Tuam, your sowl, has tuck his pasthoral staff in his hand and beathen them out o' Connaught as fast ever Pathrick druve the sarpints into Clew Bay. Poor ould Mat Kavanagh, if he was alive this day, 'tis he would be the happy man. "My curse upon their g'ographies and Bibles," he used to say; "where's

the use ov perplexing the poor childer wid what
we don't undherstand ourselves?" no use at all, in
troth, and so I said from the first myself. Well,
thank God and his Grace, we'll have no more
thrigonomethry nor scripther in Connaught. We'll
hould our lodges every Saturday night, as we used
to do, wid our chairman behind the masther's
desk, and we'll hear our mass every Sunday morning wid the blessed priest standing afore the same.
I' wisht to goodness I hadn't parted wid my Seven
Champions ov Christendom and Freney the Rob-
ber; they're books that'll be in great requist in
Leithrim as soon as the pasthoral gets wind. Glory
be to God! I've done wid their lecthirs—they may
all go and be d——d wid their consumption and
production. I'm off to Tullymactaggart before
daylight in the morning, where I'll thry whether a
sod or two o' turf can't consume a cartload ov
heresy, and whether a weekly meeting ov the lodge
can't produce a new thayory ov rints. But afore I
take my lave ov you, I may as well finish my
story about poor Father Tom that I hear is coming up to whale the heretics in Adam and Eve
during the Lint.

The Pope—and indeed it ill becomes a good Catholic to say anything agin him—no more would I, only that his Riv'rence was in it—but you see that the fact ov it is, that the Pope was as envious as ever he could be, at seeing himself sacked right and left by Father Tom, and bate out o' the face, the way he was, on every science and subjec' that was started. So, not to be outdone altogether, he says to his Riv'rence, "You're a man that's fond ov the brute crayation, I hear, Misther Ma-guire?"

"I don't deny it," says his Riv'rence; "I've dogs that I'm willing to run agin any man's, ay, or to match them agin any other dogs in the world for genteel edication and polite manners," says he.

"I'll hould you a pound," says the Pope, "that I've a quadhruped in my possession that's a wiser baste nor any dog in your kennel."

"Done," says his Riv'rence, and they staked the money.

"What can this larned quadhruped o' yours do?" says his Riv'rence.

"It's my mule," says the Pope, "and if you were to offer her goolden oats and clover off the

meadows o' Paradise, sorra taste ov aither she'd
let pass her teeth till the first mass is over every
Sunday or holiday in the year."

"Well, and what 'ud you say if I showed you
a baste of mine," says his Riv'rence, "that, in-
stead ov fasting till first mass is over only, fasts
out the whole four-and-twenty hours ov every
Wednesday and Friday in the week as reg'lar as a
Christian?"

"Oh, be aisy, Misther Maguire," says the
Pope.

"You don't b'lieve me, don't you?" says his
Riv'rence; "very well, I'll soon show you whether
or no," and he puts his knuckles in his mouth,
and gev a whistle that made the Pope stop his
fingers in his ears. The aycho, my dear, was
hardly done playing wid the cobwebs in the cor-
nish, when the door flies open, and in jumps
Spring. The Pope happened to be sitting next
the door, betuxt him and his Riv'rence, and, may
I never die, if he didn't clear him, thriple crown
and all, at one spang. "God's presence be about
us!" says the Pope, thinking it was an evil spirit
come to fly away wid him for the lie that he had

tould in regard ov his mule (for it was nothing
more nor a thrick that consisted in grasing the
brute's teeth): but, seeing it was one ov the great-
est beauties ov a grayhound that he'd ever laid his
epistolical eyes on, he soon recovered ov his fright,
and began to pat him, while Father Tom ris and
went to the sideboord, where he cut a slice ov
pork, a slice ov beef, a slice ov mutton, and a
slice ov salmon, and put them all ón a plate the-
gither. "Here, Spring, my man," says he, setting the plate down afore him on the hearthstone,
"here's your supper for you this blessed Friday
night." Not a word more he said nor what I tell
you ; and, you may believe it or not, but it's the
blessed truth that the dog, afther jist tasting the
salmon, and spitting it out again, lifted his nose
out o' the plate, and stood wid his jaws wathering,
and his tail wagging, looking up in his Riv'rence's
face, as much as to say, "Give me your absolution, till I hide them temptations out o' my
sight."

"There's a dog that knows his duty," says his
Riv'rence; "there's a baste that knows how to
conduct himself aither in the parlor or the field.

You think him a good dog, looking at him here; but I wisht you seen him on the side ov Slieve-an-Eirin! Be my soul, you'd say the hill was running away from undher him. Oh I wisht you had been wid me," says he, never letting on to see the dog at all, "one day, last Lint, that I was coming from mass. Spring was near a quarther ov a mile behind me, for the childher was delaying him wid bread and butther at the chapel door; when a lump ov a hare jumped out ov the planta-tions ov Grouse Lodge and ran acrass the road; so I gave the whilloo, and knowing that she'd take the rise ov the hill, I made over the ditch, and up through Mullagheashel as hard as I could pelt, still keeping her in view, but afore I had gone a perch, Spring seen her, and away the two went like the wind, up Drumrewry, and down Cloo-neen, and over the river, widout his being able ons't to turn her. Well, I run on till I came to the Diffagher, and through it I went, for the wa-ther was low and I didn't mind being wet shod, and out on the other side, where I got up on a ditch, and seen sich a coorse as I'll be bound to say was never seen afore or since. If Spring turned that hare ons't that day, he turned her fifty times, up and down, back and for'ard throughout and about. At last he run her right into the big quarryhole in Mullaghbawn, and when I went up to look for her fud, there I found him sthretched on his side, not able to stir a foot, and the hare lying about an inch afore his nose as dead as a door-nail, and divil a mark ov a tooth upon her. Eh, Spring, isn't that thrue?" says he. Jist at that minit the clock sthruck twelve, and, before you could say thrap-sticks, Spring had the plateful ov mate consaled. "Now," says his Riv'rence, "hand me over my pound, for I've won my bate fairly."

"You'll excuse me," says the Pope, pocketing his money, "for we put the clock half an hour back, out ov compliment to your Riv'rence," says he, "and it was Sathurday morning afore he came up at all."

"Well, it's no matther," says his Riv'rence, putting back his pound-note in his pocket-book, "only," says he, "it's hardly fair to expect a brute baste to be so well skilled in the science ov chronology."

In troth his Riv'rence was badly used in the

8

same bate, for he won it clever; and, indeed, I'm
afraid the shabby way he was thrated had some
effect in putting it into his mind to do what he
did. "Will your Holiness take a blast ov the
pipe?" says he, dhrawing out his dhudeen.

"I never smoke," says the Pope, "but I haven't
the laste objection to the smell ov the tobaccay."

"Oh, you had better take a dhraw," says his
Riv'rence, "it'll relish the dhrink, that 'ud be too
luscious entirely, widout something to flavor it."

"I had thoughts," said the Pope, wid the laste
sign ov a hiccup on him, "ov getting up a broiled
bone for the same purpose."

"Well," says his Riv'rence, "a broiled bone
'ud do no manner ov harm at this present time; but
a smoke," says he, "'ud flavor both the divil and
the dhrink."

"What sort o' tobaccay is it that's in it?" says
the Pope.

"Raal nagur-head," says his Riv'rence; "a
very mild and salubrious spacies ov the philo-
sophic weed."

"Then, I don't care if I do take a dhraw," says
the Pope. Then Father Tom held the coal him-

self till his Holiness had the pipe lit; and they sat
widout saying anything worth mentioning for about
five minutes.

At last the Pope says to his Riv'rence: "I
dunna what gev me this plaguy hiccup," says he.
"Dhrink about," says he—"Begorra," he says,
"I think I'm getting merrier nor's good for me.
Sing us a song, your Riv'rence," says he.

Father Tom then sung him Monatagrenoge and
the Bunch o' Rushes, and he was mighty well
pleased wid both, keeping time wid his hands, and
joining in the choruses, when his hiccup 'ud let
him. At last, my dear, he opens the lower buttons
ov his waistcoat, and the top one ov his waistband,
and calls to Master Anthony to lift up one ov the
windys. "I dunna what's wrong wid me, at all at
all," says he, "I'm mortial sick."

"I thrust," says his Riv'rence, "the pasthry that
you ate at dinner hasn't disagreed wid your Holiness's stomach."

"Oh my! oh!" says the Pope, "what's this at
all?" gasping for breath, and as pale as a sheet,
wid a could swate bursting out over his forehead,
and the palms ov his hands spread out to catch the

air. "Oh my!—oh my!" says he, "fetch me a basin!—Don't spake to me. Oh!—oh!—blood alive!—Oh, my head, my head, hould my head!—oh!—ubh!—I'm poisoned!—ach!"

"It was them plaguy pasthries," says his Riv'-rence. "Hould his head hard," says he, "and clap a wet cloth over his timples. If you could only thry another dhraw o' the pipe, your Holi-ness, it 'ud set you to rights in no time."

"Carry me to bed," says the Pope, "and never let me see that wild Irish priest again. I'm poisoned by his manes—ubplsch!—ach!—ach! —He dined wid Cardinal Wayld yesterday," says he, "and he's bribed him to take me off. Send for a confissor," says he, "for my latther end's approaching. My head's like to split—so it is!— Oh my! oh my!—ubplsch!—ach!"

Well, his Riv'rence never thought it worth his while to make him an answer; but, when he seen how ungratefully he was used, afther all his throuble in making the evening agreeable to the ould man, he called Spring, and put the but-end ov the second bottle into his pocket, and left the house widout once wishing "Good-night, an' plaisant dhrames to you;" and, in troth, not one of *them* axed him to lave them a lock ov his hair.

That's the story as I heard it tould; but myself doesn't b'lieve over one-half ov it. Howandiver, when all's done, it's a shame, so it is, that he's not a bishop this blessed day and hour: for, next to the goiant ov St. Jarlath's, he's out and out the cleverest fellow ov the whole jing-bang.

www.ingramcontent.com/pod-product-compliance
Lightning Source LLC
Chambersburg PA
CBHW021516090426
42739CB00007B/645